Welcome Book 4
Introduction

In the Welcome Series you will find poems
which amuse, inspire and uplift,
or which will enhance your appreciation of
the countryside.
There is also poetry which is
thought - provoking or energising.
There are verses that reflect the good deeds
done by others; in fact,
poems for every mood.
Enjoy !

Writer Anne E. Nixon

Cover Picture:
Gillian Rose Peace

000000446370

WELCOME BOOK Series 4
© Gillian Rose Peace
© Photography Gillian Rose Peace

First impression 2004
ISBN 1-897641-05-2

BRITISH LIBRARY CATALOGUING-IN-PUBLICATION DATA.
A CATALOGUE RECORD FOR THIS BOOK IS AVAILABLE
FROM THE BRITISH LIBRARY.

LIBRARY OF CONGRESS-IN-PUBLICATION DATA.

Published by :   Gill's Verse Publications
                   1, Lincomb Lock, Titton,
                   Stourport-Upon-Severn
                   Worcestershire,
                   ENGLAND
                   DY13 9QR
                   Tel: 01562 637353
                   mobile: 0770 923 9490

Printed by: Cambrian Printers
                   Llanbadarn Road,
                   Aberystwyth,
                   Ceredigion SY23 3TN
                   WALES
                   Tel: 01970 627111
                   Fax: 01970 615497

Contents

With One Look	1	The Bloom Is On The Gorse Again	27
Hope Spreads Its Light	2	Compassion	28
If With Prayer You Set Sail	3	The Hand Of Destiny	29
Who Could It Be?	4	Free As The Cat	30
The Best Actress Nominee	5	The Calming Influence	31
How Dull This World Would Be	6	Patch The Poet	32
Like a Duck Out of Water	7	Little Princess	33
Rhododendrons	8	Look At The Time And The Babby Not Washed	34
Here, Now, Mine	9	Never Leave It To Fate	35
The Scene Painter	10	There Is A World Of Dreams	36
The Old Nail Shop	11	The Spirit Of A Child	37
The Lapwing Has Returned	12	Take On Someone Your Own Size	38
God Is The Friend Of Silence	13	A Shakespearean Teddy Bear?	39
Cowslip	14	Yours Is The Choice	40
The Charmer	15	Distance Lends Enchantment	41
The Chalk Stream	16	Look To Him And Be Radiant	42
The Clock Setter	17	There's Gold In Them There Hills	43
Magnetism	18	The Pull	44
Flotilla	19	Forgive My Lapse	45
The Balance	20	A Cheerful Giver	46
Luscious Lips	21	Adjust Your Sights	47
Modern Horsepower	22	Before The Last Bus Home	48
Under The Weather	23	Classical Child	49
What Tempts Us Forth?	24	The Love Of My Life Was Mine	50
The Fallow Deer	25	The Helmsman	51
Making Sense Of It	26	At Last	52

With One Look

With one look I can win your heart
all I need is the cash to start.
Silent verses begin to flow
then back to the printers I go.
Yes, so many golden poems from my pen
here they are again.
And these words I write are here in black and white
to match the picture that's just right!

Hope Spreads Its Light!

There's always a new star on the horizon, there's always
tomorrow to live for. Hope spreads its light over all and
Nanny could call... In fact, she's here at the door!
Nanny I love you, come inside, come near – I am your
Granddaughter dear... You know I love you heaps –
that's why I call you Gillian Roast Beef!

(True Story)
(No airs and graces when children are around!)

If With Prayer You Set Sail

Compass-less across our wide expanse of sea;
with only Faith accompanying thee.
No barque will prove too frail,
If with prayer you set sail...
For prayer, like a bird following in your ship's white wake,
is always there for your loving sake.
And one prayer to many can lead;
thus a fleet of energy reveal...
Willing hope, joy, love,
upon a lucky breeze –
in which to build your dreams.

Who Could It Be?

I had to photograph this view when I recently dropped by in
Chicago (as you do). Naturally I was excited by this stretch
limo... After all Oprah Winfrey could step out - Chicago
is the home of her Harpo Studio and opposite she owned a
Condo (That's an apartment to those who don't know...) It could
be, who knows who it would be? Yes, I had to photograph this
view - but alas, it was nobody WE KNEW on Wobash Avenue!

Chicago a hell of a town!

The Best Actress Nominee...

"Life begins at forty,' I say. I remember all my lines
and haven't lost any memory. Plus my chin hasn't started
to droop, thankfully.... Naturally my star must ascend instead
of the usual descendency. I always fight for roles and my
cause - usually ending up to the sound of applause...

Yes, I'm a great actress of the silver screen, always casting
aside negative thought - and my face hasn't been cosmetically
transformed!

*This is me after I'd just played Maid Marion in an MGM
blockbuster. Nobody can believe I'm 102 years of age.*

How Dull This World Would Be

How dull this world would be if we were all "Yes" people
with no chance of expanding our view. If we limit our
conversation to please another – they'll soon become bored
with you! Successful relationships don't rely on always
trying to please – teamwork means you are special at just
being YOU. Therefore, "To your own self be true..."
Never be afraid to say you disagree – it's that something
individual about you and me!

Like a Duck Out Of Water
(Penguin version)

"I feel like a duck out of water", we often say when we've
broken from our usual routine... We feel lost and it's
something we can't quite explain... The things we do on a
daily basis become part of us. And somehow, in them, we
place our trust. If a task isn't done, that's normally done,
it seems frustrated and unsettled we become... But remember,
if the pattern of life becomes disorientated through no
fault of your own – make it a habit to pray. Especially if
done at the commencement of the day it will always keep you
safely on track... For prayer is something upon which you
can always fall back!

Rhododendrons!

Here they are again – rhododendrons! Of such bright
colour – how they bring joy into our lives – gladdening
the heart of any downhearted soul... Suddenly upliftment
hits you in the eyes, bright ball gowns of
the garden – making us again feel whole!

The Dorothy Clive Garden,
Near Market Drayton, Shropshire.

Here, Now, Mine...

You were like a prize that I secretly had to look at
With that glow of inner satisfaction;
a treasure that I'd always wanted – and now had won!
Your every intimate pleasantry caused such a virtuous sensation of
self-accomplishment;
how could I not try to relive each moment over and over –
that which was heaven sent?
Ah! In all its glorious infancy –
our mutual instinctive complacency...
perceived to us at an earlier time,
Here, now, mine!

The Scene - Painter

One part of the sky is blue, one is grey, and there are
tinges of mauve – delicate touches here and there. Wisps
like chartered ships en route to the regatta of clouds...
And mingling into them are amethyst and crimson colours –
bright scimitars that possess our eyes. Ah! the Scene - Painter
loves to adorn His canvass; and however poor a man may be –
yet look to the skies... God is there through sunset and sunrise.

The Old Nail Shop

Do we really know how our ancestors lived when we consider the cold
endurance of their lives? Did thoughts of wrong enter into their minds?
Or did they resign themselves, "To things as they are" in such a cheerless
clime? My father said, "They don't know they're born these days". And
consider what trouble-torn mother worried over her ill-fed babe?
Sickness and loss was the price so regularly paid. The grey hour fulfilling
the sameness of living... Beer was the only means of escape and so the
roaring drunkard came home with nothing to spare for others' needs.
Logic less all labour must have seemed – without a dream to dream. The
day ending forever the same by the fire's flame...
In such a brevity of life and the blight of decay in the buildings all around
– where the houses have now crumbled to the ground, we should revere
those who have gone before; for our lives are so alien to theirs, yet we do
not even think or care. Forgotten are they who first gave us air. The
levelled Churchyard we pass by, without a single sigh. And escapes not a
tear for our ancestors of yester-year.

The Old Nail Shop
Black Country Archive Photograph

The Lapwing Has Returned

The Lapwing has returned but you will never more come.
So you see, within my heart every singing bird is dumb...
How I miss those brown eyes! Happy, laughing, beneath
poppy coloured Summer skies... And walking those same old
highways now – nettles seem to edge the way of those once
happy vales... So too, I still hear the bells in each
ancient foxglove bob; but now they talk to me of days that
used to be. Too bright, too grand, is nature all around
for me to see. For what was mine has now become a cross –
the bitter one of loss.

Every Spring flower once more renews its power. Birds circle
and migrate from the seas – but you do not come back to me.
The Lapwing has returned, but not the love I thought was
mine forever.

God Is The Friend Of Silence

How we love the silence of the countryside after the noise
of the city! The branches of the trees swaying, the grasses blowing,
the lake rippling...
We gain so much from their silent beauty.
Yet there is no greater inner peace than that which prayer can give;
and yet forgetting, our rushing busy lives we continue to live...
How foolish we are and never seem to learn that we can only really
grow inwardly from quiet moments.
As the moon and stars pass quietly above, God's greatest
blessing to us comes through silent prayer –
His communication link always there.
Prayer is that silent voice within that is our permanent
guide through the storms and trials of life –
making us feel truly alive and free from strife.

He cannot be in the noisy whirl and bustling activity of the world.
Remember, God is the Friend of Silence.

Cowslip

Oops! I put me foot on the fence
to take a casual rest,
but this cow came by.
And it's no lie;
she mistook me foot for something tasty –
then realised her decision quite hasty,
and quickly sauntered away...
I wonder if she still tastes it today?

The Charmer

Displaying in immaculate modesty my feathered white pants —
you must agree I enhance... It's not surprising I'm the
Casanova of the farm and that the female owls love my
charms...

Ray's Farm, Cleobury Mortimer, Shropshire

The Chalk Stream

Here, in England's rich moving tapestry scene, fringed
with reeds — are mallard, moorhen and tufted duck;
tiny galleon ships amongst great drifts of buttercup...
And at intervals along the banks, are flanks of willows
in enchanting sway; ah! the Constable clouds are sailing
over the Wiltshire Downs today... And trancelike, I watch
the white-legged damselfly, where clear water reveals the
rainbow trout — as she weaves underwater ripples and in
her diving-dress dances about.

The Clock-Setter

I cannot add another hour to our time, I cannot write
another letter – though none ever wrote you better...
All things are published and writ as and when inspiration
dictated it... I cannot turn back the clock – though past
images go by – and our Autumn chapter leaves me with a sigh...
Oh, could we not tell when passion ran too high? That we
could not fulfil that cloud-built endeavour – promised in
such a fever? Ah! where was the future sign – when love
had seemed so aligned?

Now to dream is too late – for the clock-setter dictates.
And nothing will ever change the love eclipsed with age...

Magnetism

What is the magnetic force that love uses —
compelling us with full devotion to pursue through-out
our life a love so true... To travel miles, to cross seas,
an instinct to realize. Ah! the natural impulse, the blind
tendency to follow wherever the loved one is — because
without them life is hollow. In bliss to lavish our thoughts
on one; to carry on in deed and word the feeling that love
has stirred... For just as the poppy's flower stands out amidst
the corn — the rich scintillation of love brightens our way
from the day that it is born... Earth-bound and yet not, the
itinerant thoughts ever lead back for love's sweet honey drops.
For when eyes have met eyes — they cannot be forgot.

Flotilla

The swans today are like a flotilla of ships —
so graceful and serene, there is no finer scene...
Like a phantom fleet soon to disappear -
but could we ever forget through the years?
Though the landscape changes some things remain,
beauty in memory again...
The gleam on the water, the magical sight,
a spiritual unison of delight...

Worcester

The Balance

How steady is the rock upon which you stand? How firm the foot
on your own pathway of inner accomplishment? Remember, with God
you can make a mutual covenant... Your determining way can never
be destroyed if in God you trust – remember Faith will never be
void! God balances all things along the journey you take – the
one your soul, and your soul alone will shape... So stand tall,
give your all, and through your inner power – God will raise your
hopes that liken to a tower!

Bridgnorth Castle, Shropshire

Luscious Lips

You must admit — I have *the* most luscious lips.
I don't need any liposuction as you can see,
And all the other cows just love me!

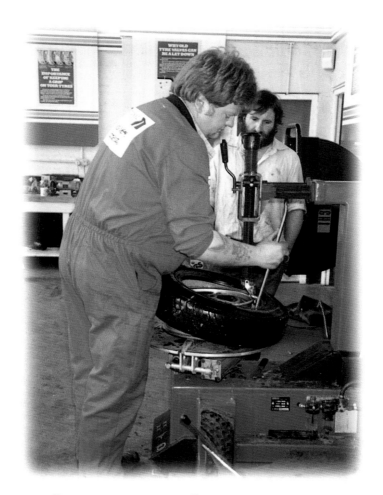

Modern Horsepower

I'm so tired of changing my treads! Tired of running around
and wearing them thin. You'd never think I walked sometimes...
A block or two, but then, I do use my car – she takes me quite
far. I'd never be without her though she takes all my money
and it's really not funny, for if it isn't the juice, there's
a screw or two loose ... A starter motor, a radiator, a clutch –
or just a touch of oil... It all makes my blood boil!
And the treads! If this is modern horsepower, then give me a
horse. Sat astride my stallion I'd look a fine woman of course...
And instead of thinking, "I've got to give it a drop of oil" –
I'd give it water from a pail... Nothing as common as "Another
re-mould please!" would pass my lips, as along her Majesty's
Highway I would trip.

Having Another Tyre Change

Under The Weather

Blimey! I know where the expression "Feeling under the
weather" comes from! How can you be cheerful when the sky is
so black? What I'd give to be on a sun-soaked beach lying
on me back... When its cold and dull I have to stick indoors –
instead of hearing happy birds sing across the moors.
The weather affects them too, it's true. There's not a sound
when the weather's bad, but once the sun is out it's like an
operatic chorus gone mad. Oh, yes, all creatures love the
sun, maybe not the polar bear, but it could melt some ice
and then a fish he'd entice...

What Tempts Us Forth?

Why must we always be active to keep us in a state of rest?
By what emotion alas, is each of us obsessed? Why do we think
to sit and do naught is not playing the part – in this our
place under the stars? Destination, course and goal in sight –
we are not happy unless in some ambitious tunnel struggling
for the light! Like a Poet ill at ease unless he writes a
terrific metaphor at speed... Instead of always chasing around
why can't we confer upon ourselves a degree – to rest, relax
and just sip tea...?

(Where someone has been enjoying a relax)
"Nasturtiums" by Stephen J Darbishire
Courtesy Stephen Darbishire Picture Library, Kendal, Cumbria

The Fallow Deer

The Fallow deer in yonder wood still grazes, he does not
know how I miss to hear your praises, and when with you I
used to walk through fields of Summer corn to the river's
reedy banks. My love with you I was ever enthralled. So long
we sat, time we forgot till the Bittern called... With his
signalling the day was ending. So little time it seemed we
had. Of that time, at least, we should be glad. But the
dandelion's clock the wind has blown – leaves one tentative
stalk. It equals the length of the time that was ours...
O, fates! Bittern you should'na have called.

In the grounds of Woburn Abbey, Bedfordshire

Making Sense Of It

In today's world of noise and confusion, bustle and speed –
how can we continue to cope? It seems we are battling for
survival in a galaxy on a collision course without hope...
What has happened to the true vision we need? Is it completely
lost in greed? Are we so programmed that we can never 'switch off'?
We ourselves choose what sense we make of it – we CAN
stop the clock. So bypass the bombardment – by carefully
choosing a more spiritual environment.

As the Poet says, "It is in the end, we who give the rose its
scent and the nightingale its song..." So don't leave it too long.

In the peace and quiet of Badger, Shropshire

The Bloom Is On The Gorse Again

The bloom is on the gorse again and reminds me everywhere
of one I used to know; alas, alas, a century ago!
Flourishing amidst hills and commons where arm in arm
we used to meet – the countryside to greet... But
there's been a death in meadow and in lane for you
and I no longer stroll where love was captured –
never to return again. Yet our best moments I still see
whenever the gorse beckons to me.

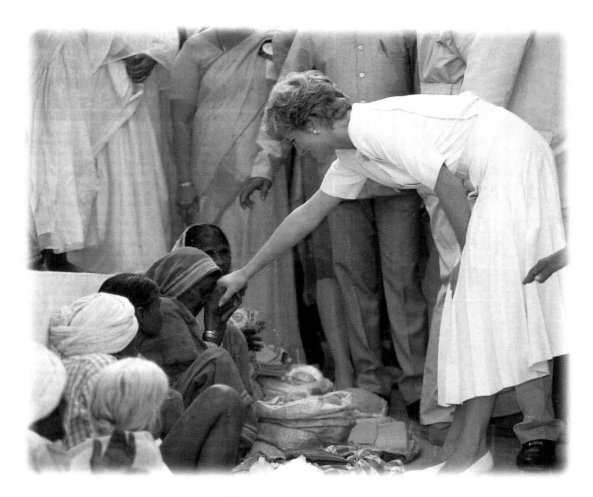

Compassion

Goodness is richer than greatness; it is not the outward thing we do but the inward person we are. It is good to be clever, to be talented, but to have compassion is greater by far... For nothing makes you truly great like being truly good. The world needs people who are always searching for ways to help others. Compassion, it says in the dictionary, is "someone who suffers inside for another", a friend who has understood... The world is filled with unkindness, but in every direction you look there is someone working quietly with love and compassion... They are the Angels of this earth administering to God's creatures, the lonely or forgotten. They, the ones who hold the Keys to the Kingdom of Heaven.

She always reached out to touch.
Poem originally written for Princess Diana who wrote back thanking me.

The Hand Of Destiny

It seems unknowingly we bid all in life that happens to us.
The weaknesses that bring our downfall at times are fixed
and set no matter what reveries we behest... For we are
ruled at birth by the planets – no matter what charms or
amulets we care to use. Our special virtues – conferred upon our
character – are blessings indeed to out-weigh unwanted
disconcerting ways. They help us through those tangled
pathways...

The ancient route of our ancestors passes down – and those
haunted out-flickering shadows inherited by none but me are
given by the Hand of Destiny.

Free As The Cat

Oh, to be as free as the cat! To roam and return
to rest at will. To find a place on sunny window sill or by
crackling fire... Tamed tiger, that too is my desire!
How my clinging cares would disappear if my approach to life
were such as yours. But I love your gentle softness as at
night across my breast you lie; those healing purrs all
stress mends – as your listless effort to me attends...

Kitty Peace

The Calming Influence

How I love the calming influence of these days – they never seem to come enough... Driving out into the countryside with you and finding an idyllic spot... With just our books for company, a hill or two to admire; pleasant bird song and an occasional church spire... These are the times of inspiration that beckon to me in other unresting days – Oh, to be a habitant of country lanes! The meadows green are filled with peace, and the sheep so contently graze... They know all Heaven is here and resign their simple nature to the fact – teaching me the humbleness I lack... Oh, how I love the calming influence of these days, they never seem to come enough.

Patch The Poet

I've never been a Poet for tragedy. I much prefer quips
and novelty... From my readers I seek favour, (they love
a good joke-maker...) Life's too short for complicated
bards with words out of the ark. High-in-the-air Poets who
think they're above the rest – when actually they're going
beyond other's depths... Oh, give me a simple line
and sincere true friends win. Verse in which no art has been
devised – brings forth applause from loved-ones' eyes.

("Although I'm American Gillian Rose loves my Pose _'er English Prose")

Little Princess

Can this really be me? Crowned as beautiful as a Princess
can be? Diamonds and pearls, jewels on my fingers as if
presented from Earls. (They all go with my golden curls...)
I can hardly wait for my Coronation to come, four white
horses my carriage will pull... Mum says, Disney will
want me, a contract I'll sign; but he better be quick – I'll
miss playtime!

Look At The Time And The Babby Not Washed!

Look at the time and the babby not washed!
I hope she won't scream and shout 'cos her dinner's
not out... But the Mother-in-law she'll have a fit —
'cos 'ers a different kettle of fish!

Old English Expression!

Never Leave It To Fate

Never leave it to fate when there's something you want in life.
Never leave it to fate and hope everything will turn out right...
Too many things will stand in your way, too many dreams will be scattered away –
if you leave it to fate.

In the battle for winning you have to be tough; prayer on its
own is never enough. For work is a blessing that you should
never hate; no one anywhere gets life on a plate... So call
upon all your endeavours – the truest and best. Goals cannot
be reached without extra zest. The success you'll achieve on
your own brings a joy that is great... Far, far better than
to leave it to fate.

Las Vegas

There Is A World Of Dreams

There is a world of dreams where you linger when absent
far beyond my call. In sleep and waking – an intangible
homesickness seems to come... An element vast and dumb.
And with clasping joy your heart I seek in all things
lovely, in all things meek. The honeysuckle drowsed with
bees; swallows darting betwixt cloud and trees... Ah!
the music of your soul murmurs in all beauty I have known;
and I have not lived this life alone.

Himley Hall Park, Himley, West Midlands

The Spirit Of A Child

Who touches the soul of a child whereby they are not
afraid to venture forth and get into all sorts of
mischief and wiles? And saying the first thing that comes
into their head, all truth prevails. For a child has no
barrier within that makes them disguise... Alien to them
is the thought of adulthood in this transitory time in
their lives. The adventure goes on forever; whether to
climb a gate and run across fields or sandy beaches to
the waves of the sea — the spirit of a child is eternal and free!

"Take On Someone Your Own Size"

"Now listen, I'm a goose, and no bull is going to act
foot loose... No lowering of the head in bossy fashion –
I'm a gander full of fighting passion!"

Ludstone Lake, Shropshire

A Shakespearean Teddy Bear?

Fancy this fine teddy bear character outside a Stratford
shop! He looks a happy soul – I bet if Dame Judi Dench
saw him she'd offer him a role!

Stratford Upon Avon, Warwickshire

Yours Is The Choice

In following the pathway I should take through life —
the Saviour always gave me a choice... I could choose the
straight and narrow — where footsteps led to no sorrow —
or I could wander the road that was open wide where He did
not promise to always be at my side... Selfishly I chose
the wrong path and wandered far — guided by my own thoughts
following the stars. When miserable and unhappy I became I
remembered that I'd made my choice — and that God forces
no one. (But I was the one to get the out-come) And I learned
that in His wisdom how wise our Saviour is in telling of the
narrow way. For there our footsteps would never stray — if we
remembered to ask His guidance and to pray.

In the grounds of Powis Castle, Mid Wales

Distance Lends Enchantment

Distance lends enchantment, and it is certainly true as we
look at a faraway horizon with its inviting hue... How easy for us to dream that life
would be different — as we gaze upon that scene of enchantment! But would it
really be so I wonder when we finally reach that dreamed of place. A new broom
may sweep clean, but after awhile we'd awaken from our dream. For no matter
where we are we'd still be the same old us; and just as easily we could get into a rut!

Enchantment is in the distance; to be looked at and admired, but real happiness is
hiding somewhere just inside... For if we put it in our pockets and take it wherever
we roam — we'd find that rainbow's end was all the time at Home.

Kephalonia, Greek Islands

Look To Him, And Be Radiant

In the Bible we read, "Look to Him, and be radiant".
Put your attitude to life under the spiritual microscope
and take a good look. Discover how lucky you are and be
grateful. Fight against despair and strive harder to retain
God's spirit with prayer... When you are depressed, look
around more positively at life and feel blessed!

Little Italy, Las Vegas

"There's Gold In Them There Hills..."

This view to me is like a beautiful painting – the Winery and
the rolling green hills of California. I could look at this scene
forever it seems. It's been said, "There's gold in them there hills",
but who needs to search? The Goldsmith has given us what we see –
a rich, beautiful earth...

Near San Francisco

The Pull

The bee has just entered a foxglove bell; and every butterfly in its own temple dwells. What mind energy draws us to its own vibrational level? The cat to the mouse, the dog to the cat; the magnetic waves that lead the pigeons back...? And the writer who cannot live without his writing? What is the pull to record every visible thing? Just like the wildebeest running and running with no end in sight — the writer has to continue to write! The crashing waves to the shore — oh, who is the Master of every living law? The gradual passing of youth to old age — tho' we try hard to evade... The electrical impulse of earth's wiles — that to every living thing beguiles!

Max amongst the foxgloves looking at the neighbour's cat!

Forgive My Lapse...

Forgive me, my child, I'm usually a creature of decorum, being chief stag of the herd – but your food is quite delicious so I've heard... I'm merely pending settlement of garnishing my mouth – so please don't think I'm being rude with my pink tongue sticking out!

Nr Bridgnorth, Shropshire
*(Photo taken by **4 year** old Bethany Egginton)*

A Cheerful Giver

How we all love a cheerful giver!
Someone who doesn't begrudge what he gives away to
another.... We don't really welcome the helping hand
when it comes because it should;
If it doesn't come with love then the giver hasn't
really understood.... That 'Giving' means so much more
than more gestures they feel they have to do; for
when we give with gladness we'll see our gift will
enrich us too... Coming back in a myriad of unexpected
ways.... Discovering the miracle that heart's gifts never fade.

Helping Nanny out of her deck chair
(To Elizabeth who always cared)

Adjust Your Sights!

Adjust your sights - look to the right - 'tis
there you'll find the light!
You are the magic answer; don't you know heaven's
face is ever there - through the frost and fog you
bear? Don't travel a million miles downcast - as if
with a burdensome pack on your back. There are
higher spiritual tracks ... In your heart is the person you want
to become; so don't let the shadows
overcome! Remember, the sun comes out and shadows
divide - it is for YOU to decide!

Blackpool Fun Fair, Lancashire

Before The Last Bus Home...

I tried to fill my life with much to gain – over-taking everyone in the outside lane. I had no time – no time to spare – filling life with all it held – breezing the air... Ambition's seeds were sown long ago in youth. I planned a million things to do in truth. I had the energy and God was on my side – I'd take it in my stride! Practical opinions meant nothing to my purposings – and how they loved to mention those purse strings! Yet we only get one chance in life, just one chance alone – before the last bus home...

Wolverhampton Roe Bodied Sunbeam Trolley Bus,
Now at the Black Country Living Museum, Dudley, West Midlands

Classical Child

I'm such a classical child. Mozart now, but the other day
I was teaching dancing to Elvis Presley. I'm a writer too
and one day I'll tell a tale or two... All this cleverness
I get from my Nan, Gillian Roast Beef – who's crossed every
Barrier Reef!

The Love Of My Life Was Mine

Beloved, there's an echoing cry within my heart
that comes and ever asks why?
Why did love come, and then go away —
why did cynic fate decree You should not stay?

Yet it is enough to know
that I am sheltered in your thoughts;
for breaking into my solitude
the remembrance will always shine,
that the love of my life was mine.

The Helmsman

All haphazard we rush through life – and then life's gone.
Why in ceaseless motion do we pursue – who
knows what, who knows who? Yet we are the Helmsman. The one who steers our
own course. We ourselves are the source... So let us slow
down along the over-brimming pathway of our lives. For only
by slowing down to a steady pace, one that is calm and serene, will you ever find
true happiness... and your dream.

Resting in the harbour, Kephalonia, Greek Islands

At Last

Tuwhit tuwhoo, who are you?
I declare, it's the famous Gillian Rose.
(She had to find me eventually, I suppose...)

Ray's Farm, Cleobury Mortimer, Shropshire